SHORTCUT TO ALASKA

10 SHORT STORIES OF SPIRITUAL INSPIRATION

BY

KATHLEEN MORRIS

Rouge Publishing

Rouge Publishing

978-1-927828-20-5

Other Books By Kathleen Morris

Deep Bay Series
Deep Bay Vengeance
Deep Bay Relic
Deep Bay Legacy (Coming 2014)

Blood War Series
The Prion Attachment
Blood Purge (Coming 2014)

Short Inspirations Series
Size Seven Shorts
Short End Of The Stick
Shortcut To Alaska

Short Stories
Along The Way - 12 Short Stories You Can Read Along
The Way

Plays
Time Will Tell - An Easter Play
Even Me - A Christmas Play For Your Sunday School
All I Need Is Love - A Play For Teens
Lost And Found - A Children's Christmas Play
Gotta Love It - A Humorous Play About Rural Life

How - To Books
How To Make Eye Catching Ebook Covers Easily

Available on Amazon.com

DEDICATION

Short Cut To Alaska is my third book in the Short Inspirations series. I wanted to write a book about the cruise to Alaska I took with my husband to celebrate our 25th anniversary. I have included ten true life stories about our adventures and the many different lessons we learned along the way.

This book is dedicated to my dearest husband Barry. *Thank you my love.*

I would also like to dedicate this book to my three children, Renee, Philip, and Brett. You have been *my blessings* in the last 25 years. If your dad and I would not have had you, we would surely be boring old people, and would never have had anyone to encourage us to go on a cruise to Alaska. *The trip of a lifetime.* Thanks kids!

Table Of Contents

The Maze...9
Love Thy Neighbour 15
All In My Head 19
Who Brought The Sun?.....................................27
Even The Ravens...31
Lost in Translation 37
Your Diamonds 41
Watching Paint Dry 45
The Last Flight Home 51
Twirl..59
ABOUT THE AUTHOR......................................62

The Maze

It was the first day of our trip and a day to remember.

We hopped a plane in Saskatoon at 8 a.m and didn't look back. By the time we arrived at the Vancouver airport, we were so excited and eager to begin our cruise to Alaska. We were greeted by representatives from the Norwegian cruise lines who held a sign with our name on it, for our shuttle to the pier. It made us feel special and brought comfort because we'd never been to the Vancouver airport before, and we were first time cruisers.

Once we got to the Vancouver pier, that's when the fun began. Our memories are a bit of a fog because it happened so fast, but thinking back on it now, I remember feeling like a herd of cattle as we were lead through a large maze. Several mazes I might add.

First, when you start the boarding process of a large cruise ship, you have to go through customs and security. They combine this process with registration and there is nothing quite like it.

Yellow tape is sectioned off into many laneways, and as fast as lightening, you are led through the rows to be processed. It was fun yet overwhelming at the same time, and if you're not prepared, look out. You have to have your passport in hand and open to your picture. You also have to have your boarding passes open for registration.

It was an event I will never forget, and I call it an event because it was. Over two thousand people went through this process with us all at once, in the blink of an eye we were rushed in like a herd of cattle. But it wasn't a bad thing when I call us cattle, we were treated like purebreds at the same time.

If you try to slow down or fumble with your boarding pass or your passport isn't open properly, they tell you to hurry-up. But once we were through one maze, we were lead to yet another. We were divided into two sections: Those who had cruised before, and those who had not. We were first timers so we had to say goodbye to the regulars we had already met in the great rat race of cruisers.

Once we went through our *first timer* cruise line-up, we were rushed through the registration line. That in itself was daunting. They checked us in and gave us a key fob to our state room. Oh, we were excited, but tired as a dog. This rat race was quickly wearing us out. I shudder to think of all those unfortunate people who didn't pay for shuttle service to take their luggage ahead of time. We did. We were fortunate to have a travel agent that advised us that it would be well worth our while to purchase. It was. Thank you Jacqueline! Those people who were pulling loads of luggage behind them, were ready to fall over.

Much easier to get through the rat race without having to carry a lot of baggage.

Finally, we were processed and led to a holding pen. I call it that, because it's exactly what it felt like. The ship wasn't ready yet, and so we all sat in chairs in a large waiting area. It was stuffy and hot, and everyone around us looked like they just got the wind knocked out of them. In fact, they probably had. The processing of a cruise ship is not for the faint of heart.

Once we sat in the chairs, all two thousand of us, we finally exhaled. If you were grumpy, your experience wouldn't be as pleasant, but if you go with the flow, it can be quite entertaining. We had a lot of fun, though we were very tired. We were eager to get on board and relax, but knew it would be some time before they called our row.

The alternative to the rat race was to board at the last minute, but most didn't want to do that because they'd risk not being on board on time. If that happened, and you missed the cut off time, you simply were not allowed to cruise. That wouldn't have been a good thing, since most people pre-paid and would've lost everything. Yes, they would've let you board at the next Port, but you'd have to fork out your own money and transportation to get to Ketchikan, Alaska on your own. *That*, we wanted to avoid at all costs.

Finally, they called our row, and away we went to the gangway. It was exciting. We entered the ship as the staff greeted us with a smile and a commemorative photo. Hard to sneak by without getting your picture taken. We avoided it the first day, but found out there were many other photo opportunities whether we wanted it or not.

It was an exciting event boarding the ship to Alaska that day. One I will never forget; and the whole process reminded me a little of the way the world works. We're all caught up in the maze of life, trying to make our way in the big rat race.

I hate the rat race of life. You get up every day to head out to work, blend in with all the other cattle doing the same thing as you are, and hurry to your destination. We repeat it as we journey home, just to start it all over again the next day. *Crazy!*

At times we wonder why we keep doing it. We know there is a reason, but while in the midst of it, we forget that reason. We wish there was another way, and perhaps there is. Sometimes this alternative way is risky, so we opt out for the easy way. It's okay, and sometimes fun, but very exhausting.

It's made worse by the baggage we carry. If we have difficulty at work or home, or have bad debts, or poor health, or live in poverty, the whole process is gruelling. But if we have a positive attitude, no matter what the circumstance, we can get through it. Grumbling and complaining about the rat race only makes it worse.

I wonder what it would be like to take a detour though, I seriously do. Risk shouldn't be that scary. What if we ventured off the beaten path? What if we took another route? We might fail, but we might not.

All these questions go through my mind when thinking of the great rat race of life and the many different mazes we find ourselves in and wonder how God fits into play. Is He there prodding us on like cattle, herding us in like a rancher does? Or is He singling us out and encouraging us to find our own path?

I don't have the answers, but I do have the Bible just like everyone else. Thankfully God left us a passport. I can open it and have clear passage to any help that I need. And on this day, I chose to go to Isaiah 41:10 "*So do not fear, for I am with you; do not be dismayed, for I am your God. I will strengthen you and help you; I will uphold you with my righteous right hand."*

That verse is like a breath of fresh air to me, especially when the wind is knocked out of me. I know that whatever I'm facing in my day, God will be there right beside me helping me find my way through the maze, giving me strength to get through the rat race, and encourage me to keep on going.

And perhaps one day, I'll take the short cut instead of winding through the endless maze and find my own way, even though it's risky. A well traveled path is not the only route. Sometimes you have to venture off to sea, and risk the waves and turbulence. But it's worth it none-the-less, even though its scary. I know that God will be by my side no matter what route I take and he'll be with you too, guiding you if you ask; making sure your short cut leads you in the right direction.

Like my short cut to Alaska, a cruise of a lifetime.

Love Thy Neighbour

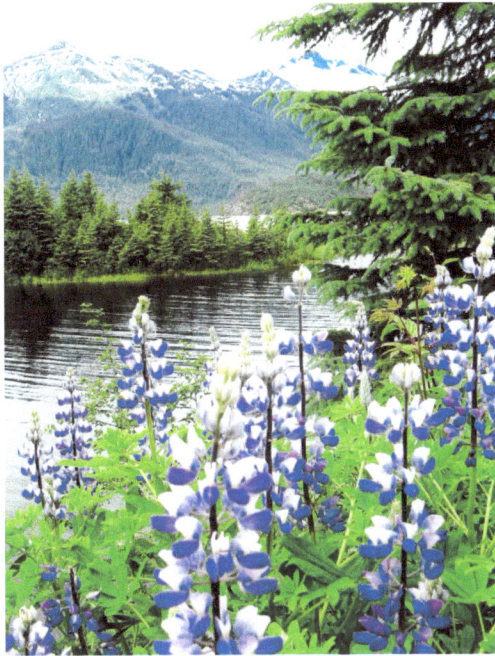

What is racism?

It's a question every person struggles with. I know I do. Do we look at someone as inferior just because they have a different colour of skin, or smell, or language?

I often hear people-bashing in every walk of life including my own mouth. How many times have I grumbled that I feel like a minority? It's just talk, we all fool ourselves, but could it possibly be the dreaded word, *racism*?

God taught me a huge lesson on my cruise to Alaska, one I will never forget. Even today it continues to impact me. It's something I never would have experience anywhere else.

Right from the start, when I boarded the giant cruise ship, I noticed I was a minority. There weren't many English speaking people on board. If I felt like a minority back home, I certainly did on the cruise ship. There were so many people from different countries. This actually intrigued me.

I met people from the Philippians, Taiwan, China, Pakistan, Italy, Germany, Australia, Canada, the U.S, and the list goes on. I thought this might become a problem at first. How could so many different ethnic people get along together on a trip to Alaska? Either we were going to completely ignore each other, or there were going to be nightly brawls, or so I thought.

It was amazing what happened next.

As we set sail, there was only one thing going on in each and every language on board: *excitement!* We were all headed to the most picturesque place in the world. It didn't matter what language we were excited in, and it didn't matter if we all understood it either. We didn't need an interpreter for that.

As the week went by, thanks to my husband the social butterfly, I met amazing people I would've never had the opportunity to meet otherwise. I'm sure I wouldn't have spoke to them if I would've met them on the street. I may have unknowingly dismissed them because of their race.

What a shame. I shake my head now. Is it really that bad that people from different ethnic backgrounds have moved into town? Is it really that bad that our jobs are being filled by people from other countries? All these thoughts now run through my mind because of what God taught me that interracial week where no boarders divided our hearts and minds.

It's how it should be.

We were all headed the same direction on a mighty cruise ship where the walls were blurred. There was no such thing as, *my side*, or *your side*. It was so pleasant and heart-warming. I wished I could bring it home with me. In a sense, I did. Too bad I couldn't bring it home for other people to share in a more concrete way besides my writing.

One group of people I really wanted to point out, is the Filipino people. I really grew to love them. They have such big hearts! The majority of the staff were from the Philippians, and for good reason: They're good at it! I was never taken better care of in my life. Everywhere my husband and I went, we were always greeted by someone who knew our name. Perhaps it was the cruise line. Norwegian Cruises are the best, but I think it's more about the people they hire. They treat you kindly, and that will never be forgotten.

Now that the cruise is done, I shake my head at how racist I really was before. Shame on me! People are people; they all love, cry, hurt, think, and feel the same as everyone else. We are all children of God and should act like it by accepting everyone else. And I'm not just talking about different races. What about those in poverty, or mentally challenged, or have physical ailments? Do we treat those people differently just because they smell different, or can't afford new clothes?

I have made it a life's quest to curb my mind from it's wayward thinking from now on. I want to smile back at a person, just because. I want to open a door for someone who can't, just because.

And the most important thing of all: I want to love because Jesus says, "The greatest of these is love!" We are to love because Christ loved us first. No more racist remarks like, "they're taking our jobs," or "they need to go back to their own country" or "Why don't they learn how to speak English?" That's just mean. Learning another language is not easy. I would find it very hard.

And the world is big, there are many languages. I don't want to be so arrogant as to think that the English language is the best and most popular. Shame on me if I do!

I'm glad God put me on that ship, if not to show me that He made a big and beautiful world of people from all walks of life, but to teach me to love. It's something to be appreciative of without condemnation.

I think of heaven and what it must be like. When we all get there, will we be broken up according to our ethnic backgrounds? I think not. We will all work together in harmony. I know it will be amazing!

We should all get along as well as we did on that cruise. The world would be a better place because of it.

So remember, as I will try to do myself: *LOVE THY NEIGHBOUR!*

All In My Head

When waves go up and down, I experience motion sickness, or sea sickness. Call it what you like, but I generally don't feel well on the ocean, or in a plane, or even riding in a car sometimes. I usc to get car sick all the time when I was little. I don't know what causes it, but it sure is nasty.

On our trip to Alaska, I didn't think I'd get seasick because I was prepared, or so I thought. I took the advice of many people who told me you don't look straight at the motion, you look past it. Well that's easy for them to say, but to someone who has that problem with any kind of motion, it ain't easy.

As soon as we boarded the ship I felt a little queasy. It was a stable vessel, and it was huge, so I thought I would be fine. As we left the Vancouver harbour, I grew more and more accepting of the home that I would be floating on for the next week. I thought I got my sea legs as some people put it, but apparently not.

The first day I was fine. I could see out the very large windows, I was doing wonderful, and we were traveling through a narrow passage with mountains on either side of us. We sat in the dining room and ate our meals no problem. Even sitting backwards against the direction we were traveling didn't bother me quite as much as I thought.

It wasn't until our safety drill that I realized I may be in big trouble. We all had to gather at our station on the main promenade deck underneath the safety boats as the staff drilled us as to the emergency protocol required if we should turn into the Titanic.

That thought in itself panicked me as I wondered about the many people who died in the Titanic and the simple fact that there wasn't enough lifeboats. Now that's the first question my husband and I asked the staff. Apparently, there were enough lifeboats, however the staff didn't seem to know how to operate the safety boats without power. Oh yes, they informed us how to turn this on and how to turn that on, but as my husband so delicately pointed out, what if the ship loses power? We were informed not to worry, that there were winches etc and we would be just fine.

I don't know if fear started my seasickness, or panic, or the fact that I just kept thinking about the Titanic. Even though I tried to keep my emotions intact, I just couldn't. I started looking around at all the other people in our station that were supposed to get on our lifeboat in the event we sink, and there was only one thing that stood out in my mind: those tiny little circular patches behind everybody's ear.

They look like bandages, so I asked the person in front of me what they were. Seasickness patches, I was told. You get them as a prescription from your doctor before you leave. *BEFORE* you leave. Apparently I was out of the loop.

Gah, I didn't know. I felt bile rising to the surface of my throat and I started to panic. Why hadn't anyone told me about this? We were told that we could go to the doctor's station on board and get seasickness pills, but not the patches. Apparently these patches were slow working and let out a little bit of medication daily so you don't toss your cookies over the side of the ship.

I silently screamed, "*HELP!*" but nobody heard me. I was just going to have to put up with whatever seasickness came my way and that was that.

Right away my husband and I headed for the doctor on board to get our seasickness pills. I don't know why I thought they were any different than the gravel pills I already had with me for just-in-case purposes, but I did. Somehow I thought that these pills the doctor was going to give would be more effective. As it turned out the doctor's line was far too long so we decided to head for our cabin and get a good nights rest without any so-called seasickness pills.

As we got ready for bed, I made the mistake of looking out of our porthole window. That's when it hit me the worst. I could see the waving water against the side of the boat and the dizziness started.

"Just go to sleep," my husband told me. "You'll feel better in the morning."

Well morning came, and I did feel much better so I thought that was it for seasickness. We went through another day going through the mountains and the inside passage and it was beautiful. No seasickness at all

The next few days were uneventful in the seasickness department. It wasn't until we headed out to open waters instead of the inside passage: The real sea. I lost my horizon and began to feel very ill while we were whale watching. I guess looking down into the water for most of the afternoon will do that to you. And when you look back up and can't find the horizon because you're in the middle of the ocean far away from land, you tend to feel sick.

From then on, I couldn't shake it. I didn't even want to see a window leave alone look out. Our favourite place to eat was at the top of the ship. There I felt fine. It was hard to even see the water below because you were so high up, and I could look into the distance a lot easier. I was told the top of the ship is the place you want to be if you feel sick.

For the most part, I tried to ignore the seasickness and really have a good time. Don't get me wrong, I did have a great time and would go on a cruise again, but not without the seasickness patches.

The last night on board was a blur to me. The ship was going full steam ahead on open water as we rushed back to Port. My tummy didn't like that very much. As my husband and I went out to dine for the very last night on board, we were offered our usual spot beside the window, but I declined.

I asked to be placed away from the window, so the gracious staff put us on the other side. Well that didn't help either. I could still see all the many windows; and I could still see the waves; and I could still feel the entire ship in motion, even though no one else could feel this motion. It was all in my head.

As the waiters arrived with our food and placed it on our table in front of us, I suddenly felt more ill than before. "I'm sorry," I told my husband, gulping back the bile, "I can't eat!"

With one final attempt to please me, the staff moved us to the very center of the dining room, and took great effort in setting up a new table for us so that I couldn't see out any windows whatsoever. But that didn't work either. I attempted to lift my fork to my mouth and just couldn't. By that time, the ship was rocking so violently in my head that I had to hang onto the table.

I felt like a crazy woman. "Can't you feel that?" I moaned to my husband.

But nobody else felt it. I was losing my mind and I was about to lose more than that if I didn't get out of there quickly. I said my goodbyes, apologize to my husband for ruining our last evening out and headed for my cabin quickly.

My poor husband followed shortly after with a armload of takeout to eat later but I didn't even want to see it or smell it. *I just wanted to die.*

I don't remember much after that. I know I was force-fed two of the doctor's seasickness pills, and that I was out like a light, but everything else was a blur. We were supposed to go to the nightly performance in the Star Dust Lounge that night to see a magician, but the only magician I saw was in my dreams. I was so drugged up that I couldn't even move my mouth or my body for that matter.

The next morning I felt much better. We were at Port and it was time to leave. Our bags had been packed the day before. My final packing was done by my husband, and it was a bit sad. Even though we spent a week on the ship and I did enjoy myself greatly with many fond memories, I felt a little cheated. I wish someone would have informed me about the seasickness patches. Perhaps they did, but knowing me, it just went in one ear and out the other.

I'll certainly know for the next time. And looking back on it all, I realize that a lot of my seasickness was brought on by fear. I was afraid of that unknown – *the what ifs*. What if we hit an iceberg like the Titanic did, and died? What if I fell overboard? What if I barfed in public? What if I got so sick I had to be flown to a hospital on land and couldn't continue on the cruise that I *already* paid for?

I believe I wouldn't have experienced seasickness as much if I would have controlled my fear. After all, it started to get worse during the emergency procedures with the life boats. And what I didn't realize at the time was that God was in control. He's always in control. How could I forget that?

Even the people on board the Titanic were in God's hands. There are many that would refute this, but I believe it. There isn't a single hour that we can add to our lives by worrying. Just as the Bible states in Ecclesiastes 3-8, *"There is a time for everything, and a season for every activity under the heavens: a time to be born and a time to die, a time to plant and a time to uproot, a time to kill and a time to heal, a time to tear down and a time to build, a time to weep and a time to laugh, a time to mourn and a time to dance, a time to scatter stones and a time to gather them, a time to embrace and a time to refrain from embracing, a time to search and a time to give up, a time to keep and a time to throw away, and a time to tear and a time to mend, a time to be silent and a time to speak, a time to love and a time to hate, a time for war and a time for peace."*

But even though I know this, I'm still afraid. Every day I have to pray and ask for God's protection. Every day I worry about all the what-ifs. But when I finally surrender it to the God who created this big world, I can be calm even though the waters are raging, even though the world is spinning. I can stand firm in my beliefs and know that *He* is my center of gravity!

ALWAYS!

Who Brought The Sun?

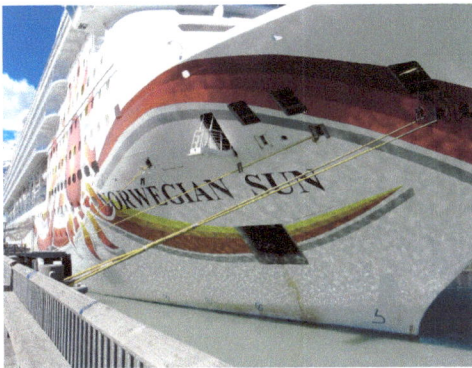

When you wake up in the morning, do you want sunshine or rain?

I actually love both, but the sunshine does bring warmth and most people love a sunny day. On our cruise to Alaska, almost ever day was sunny. We were told in Ketchikan, that *that* almost never happens. Most days are cloudy and rainy and in fact, Ketchikan is the rain capital of Alaska.

But not the week we were there.

The locals were smiling and running about their day with a little more bounce in their step, and we were told we must've brought the sun. Well, in actuality, we did bring the sun. We brought the *Norwegian Sun*, the name of our cruise ship. I'd like to think I thought of that pun myself, but I'm afraid it wasn't my wit that came up with it.

But it's true none-the-less.

Our cruise ship was one of the best looking ships as we pulled into the Ketchikan harbour that day. As we docked in the sunshiny Port, it looking wet and soggy from previous rains. We realized they hadn't seen the sun in days. That particular day it shone brilliant in the morning sun as we exited our massive ship for a day of fun and adventure.

The Norwegian Sun isn't just a ship, it was our home for a full week, and I was proud to say that I travelled on such a beautiful ship. It really was amazing inside and out: A giant white ship with a great big sun painted on its Port and Starboard side. *Spectacular!* And I just had to use the correct nautical terms to prove that I actually learnt something during the cruise and didn't put my brain on auto-pilot for the entire holiday.

Seriously though, I think of my own life and wonder if I bring the sun like we did that cheery morning in Ketchikan, Alaska. Do people feel warm around me? Do they feel the calm soothing of the sun or do I portray dismal rain? I wouldn't say that rain is a negative thing, but my point reflects *attitude.*

Attitudes can really make or break a situation. I would be proud to bring the sun into any situation and hope that by doing so, others would feel warmth around me. But, unfortunately, I fail more often than not. I complain, I blame, I make a mess of a situation many a time. I am not perfect.

Often, this it the struggle we bring into the day. It's not that we intend to do this, it just happens. Our attitudes are a direct reflection of what is going on in our lives. We might be having a difficult time at work, or our home life, or our health, that makes us miserable. We lash out at others and have a generally negative attitude sometimes. I hate it when that happens to me, and if we're honest with ourselves, that isn't the way we want to be.

So, my question to myself is how do I change this? How do others change this? How can we turn our frowns upside down so to speak? How do we bring the sun?

I like to think of the word sun as a pun. If we brought more of the *Son*, meaning *Jesus Christ* into a situation, that would bring the sun, would it not? I know I want to bring the *Son* so that the sunshine can cast a presence of happiness on all situations. Reality is, we just can't turn every situation around. That would be impossible.

But my God is in the business of doing just that. You might be suffering from depression, or a loss, or going through health problems, and wondering what I could possibly know about *your* pain. I've been in pain too, and pain is pain. I know how it can fester in people's lives and I know how hard it is to change that, and look toward the *sun/son*.

The Bible says in Psalm 97: 11-12, "*Light is shed upon the righteous and joy on the upright in heart. Rejoice in the Lord, you who are righteous, and praise his holy name.*"

At first glance you might tell yourself that God only helps the righteous and you're nowhere near that. I know, I thought that immediately. "Yeah," I told myself, "but I'm not righteous."

Then I started to wonder what righteousness really was and if I even fit the category at all. Well, according to Greek definition and how it applies to the Bible, we can conclude that righteousness means a conformity to established standards. Okay, so that to me would mean, following God. But still, that presents a question of how well we do it. If you're like me, not so well. I'm a fallible creature.

These next couple verses give me hope though. Matthew 6:33 says, "*If we put the Kingdom of righteousness in first place, then all these other things will be given to you.*" That is a huge comfort to me. It tells me that there is still hope for little old me, and for all those who struggle, because God also said in Matthew 5:6, "*Those who hunger and thirst for righteousness are blest, because they will be satisfied.*"

Well folks, I am thirsty.

All I can say, is *that* is salve to my wounds, and should be to yours as well. It means that even though we fail, and count ourselves as unworthy and unrighteous, God does not. To Him, we are righteous because we try to follow Him as best we can, and that is all that matters. *We try; I try.* I do my best to follow Him and He promises that we will be blest because of it and our reward is His *light* shed upon us.

I think of the sun, and the *Son,* and I'm thankful for both, as both play such an integral part in our wellbeing every single day. I don't want to bring a sad disposition into the day and pollute others around me with my negative attitude; I want to shine; I want the light to illuminate through me, as Christ does.

So, the next time you get up in the morning, whether you pull into an Alaskan Port on a cruise ship, or go to school, or pay the bills, or head off to work, remember to bring the sun and also bring the *Son.* It will light your day and change attitudes around you, including your own.

That, *my friends,* is the blessing!

Even The Ravens

    During a shore excursion to Juneau, Alaska we went on a tour called *Ghosts And Goodtime Girls.* It was supposed to be one of the best tours, and it certainly turned out to be. It was a tour that was guided by a so-called *goodtime* girl, led throughout the town of Juneau. We walked the streets and were told about the early colourful past of the first Juneau settlers.

Madam Ophelia was our guide and she dressed the part exactly. She led a small group of us through the streets, to banks and historical sites and told us many entertaining stories of how the town came to be. It was very enjoyable and she was a great actress.

Some of the spots she took us to were quite interesting and sent shivers up our spines. She told us ghost stories about empty abandoned homes and that got me to thinking. I've never believed in ghosts, but after hearing some of those stories, I wondered how they fit into my own spiritual beliefs.

One story in particular focused on ravens. She told us that ever since the unfortunate death of a family that lived in one of the homes, ravens had gathered. At to this day, the ravens still gather. *We saw them.*

Some say ravens are smarter than dogs and represent departed spirits. At first I didn't know what to think of this because as a Christian, that kind of thinking was generally frowned upon. But the more I thought about it, the more I wondered. And certainly, the ravens were in fact there. They seemed to only gather *there*, right in the spot where the death occurred over a hundred years ago.

Why?

Perhaps I ask why too much. Maybe I should just leave it alone, but the writer in me always wonders. I can't let it go until I pursue it further. And so I did. What I came up with was different to say the least.

Firstly, all creatures are God's creation. There isn't one that He didn't make as Colossians 1:16 states, *"For in Him all things were created: things in heaven and on earth, visible and invisible, whether thrones or powers or rulers* or authorities; all things have been created through Him and for Him."

So these large purple-black birds with glistening plumage are nothing to fear. It is man that forced that fear upon such a beautiful creature. Really, a raven is one of the most beautiful birds in the air. So why do we cast such a dark shadow on it?

I remember watching this disturbing movie called, "*Kaw*" where ravens got sick with mad cow disease and started pecking everyone to death. Now especially, when I see a raven, I duck and scream. It's a natural instinct after being told that they hold the souls of those departed and carry mad cow disease.

Our imaginations can grow by the minute.

But I'm the first to admit I have a huge imagination. I wouldn't be a writer if I didn't. But the writer in me also tells me to research and investigate further. And so I did. What I found was both encouraging and discouraging.

Firstly, ravens seem to serve a purpose both biblically and in society as a whole. They symbolize impurity. Yes, even one of God's creatures can be used in such a way. I just wondered why, so I found scripture to help me.

In Genesis 8: 6-8 it states, "*At the end of forty days Noah opened the window of the ark which He had made, and sent forth a raven; and it went to and fro until the waters were dried up from the earth. And He sent forth a dove from Him.*"

But the raven didn't do very well it seems. It didn't come back. We don't know if it didn't come back to Noah's hand directly, or if it came back to the ark but then was too smart to be tamed back into the ship. The details aren't exactly clear as to what happened, but obviously the raven symbolizes rebellion in some way or another. Perhaps ravens represent our lives without Christ, unlike the accepting dove that *did* obediently come back with an olive branch.

Many times in the Bible, a gentle dove is compared to the Holy Spirit, when a raven is compared to something that is dark, unclean, and without a soul. I think God created it like that. What a wonderful teaching tool. He can use it to teach us so much, and so He has. He used the raven to show us that we can either follow God, or follow the world.

Like a raven, independent and smart, it pecks away at anything just to survive. Mostly, it relies on itself for food, eating road kill and dead carcasses. But the Bible also says that God feeds the ravens. So...the way I look at it is, a raven is a metaphor for our own free will. We can either be dark and follow the ways of the world, completely independent of God, or, we can be obedient followers of Christ like a gentle dove, allowing the Holy Spirit to guide us. And even if we are big and dark with blue-black plumage like a raven, we don't have to live as a raven does, we can still allow God to feed us.

And how does this fit with the ghost stories we were told about in Juneau, Alaska you might ask. *Simple.* I believe that ravens are neither good nor bad but open vessels which God can use according to His purpose. Equally, in the opposite direction, the enemy has access to these creatures, and can use them for harm.

Luke 12:24 states this, "*Consider the ravens: they neither sow nor reap, they have neither storehouse nor barn, yet God feeds them. Of how much more value are you than the birds!*" That alone tells me that ravens neither sow nor reap and I take that to mean they are neutral creatures, to be used by God according to His purpose.

I can see how raven folklore speaks negatively of these birds but I think God knew what He was doing when He created them. People can think of them as evil creatures,

34

and perhaps there is some reality there. But, for me, I know that God created these birds, just like He created humanity, and it is up to us what we do with that. We can either adopt a rebellious, independent, selfish nature against God, or allow Him to feed us so that we too can be like a gentle dove.

There is hope for everyone, *even the ravens!*

Lost in Translation

Have you ever tried to have a conversation with someone from another country? It isn't the easiest thing. On our cruise to Alaska we met a couple from Rome, Italy. They had their little translation booklet out wherever they went and tried to have conversations with people even though they only spoke Italian.

It seemed everywhere we went on the ship we bumped into them, which probably wasn't a coincidence at all. God allows circumstances to teach us different things in our lives to help us grow and become the people we are today.

This was no exception. We were celebrating our 25th anniversary, and they were celebrating their honeymoon. It was quite a nice contrast. For some reason they seemed to click with us. They were both about 10 or 15 years younger than us but still we seemed to be able to have things in common.

If it wasn't for my husband Barry, I would never have muscled up the nerve to talk to people who didn't speak our language. But he was persistent, making funny motions with his hands and going over and over the words so that this young couple could understand.

I remember one afternoon we were sitting next to the large windows watching for whales, when a funny conversation took place. We were talking about how men understand things differently than women. It was difficult because they couldn't quite understand what we were saying, and we couldn't understand what they were saying, but we all understood the topic.

This young couple was trying to get their point across that a man's emotions were driven by his brain, and the guy pointed to his head as he looked up the word in his translation dictionary. We understood that quite well but couldn't understand what the woman was saying when she rubbed her *belly* and laughed that women think with that part of our anatomy.

They giggled, and we shook our heads, and neither one of us could understand the meaning of the woman as she continued to rub her belly. It was the most entertaining afternoon of the entire cruise. What they were trying to get across to us was lost in translation.

We went over some words and they shook their heads *no,* telling us that wasn't what they were talking about. They grabbed the translation dictionary again and went over what they were trying to say. Still we didn't understand. What did the woman mean as she rubbed her belly? Did she mean women were like her belly? *Huh?*

Barry questioned if she was pregnant, but they both laughed, "*no-no!*" Then tried again. It went on like this for quite a while until I finally thought about it. If men's emotions were controlled by their brains meaning they usually are not influenced by up-and-down emotions, then women are the opposite. We are controlled by our emotions, which are controlled by our *hormones.*

Bingo! I hit the nail right on the head. As soon as I said the word hormone, both the Italian woman and the Italian man shook their heads and laughed uncontrollably. "*Sì-sì*, Yes!" They both said, "*Hormone-y, Hormone-y!*" It was very funny and you had to be there to hear the whole conversation to understand it completely.

After that, we seemed to understand each other a little bit better. It doesn't matter what culture you're from or language you speak, men and women are the same everywhere.

There are so many different languages and translations in the world, I sometimes wonder if God's messages get lost in translation. We have many different translations for the Bible to begin with, and that's mostly for the English language. What about all the other languages? A simple Bible verse can so easily lose its meaning if we're not careful.

Just like the Italian woman rubbing her belly, trying to explain hormones, and us interpreting it the wrong way, the Bible is also hard to understand. When we think about the different versions, perhaps much of it is lost in translation as well.

But there's one message in the Bible that I hope will never be lost or misinterpreted, and that is *love.* No matter what type of Bible you read, or what language you speak, or what kind of ethnic background you're from, there's one message that remains clear at least to me, and that is the love that God gave us through His son Jesus Christ.

"*For God so loved the world, that He gave His only begotten son, that whosoever believeth in Him should not perish, but have everlasting life."* John 3:16 is my favourite. It's that verse that brings forth the message of love and it's importance to all humanity.

We are called to love because Christ loved us first, and that is what should bring us together not apart. It doesn't matter if we come from a Catholic background, Baptist, Pentecostal, Mennonite, Lutheran, or any other denomination. It shouldn't matter what version of the Bible we read, or what kind of traditions we follow, we are all the same and our differences shouldn't be what separate us. Our common denominator is love, and that's the only thing that should matter.

No wonder Jesus said, *"The greatest of these is love!"*
Lets make sure *love* is never lost in translation.

Your Diamonds

There's one thing you should know before you go on any cruise, and that is that the cruise lines own the jewellery stores. It's something I didn't know before hand. I just thought it was a coincidence that every Port had an abundance of jewellery stores.

Oh, the jewels were beautiful, but I was beginning to wonder if purchasing these gems was a prerequisite for returning to the ship. I was handed out so many coupon booklets for jewellery stores that I couldn't carry them all.

It's true that diamonds are a girl's best friend, but this was getting a little too much. I wondered how many diamonds a girl needed. Perhaps you can wear a ring on every finger but that would get a little bit costly for my taste. Not only that, I wouldn't want to flash that kind of *bling.*

Don't get me wrong, I'm a girl who loves *bling.* I like all kinds of jewellery from necklaces, earrings, rings, bracelets, you name it. Jewellery made by *Lia Sophia* is my absolute favourite brand and my husband knows it. He's bought me many a lovely item from that jewellery line.

I don't wear all my jewellery at once though but many people do. Each to their own, but for me, I like to wear them one at a time, and they each represent something to me. I wear my wedding ring for example, because it represents twenty-five years of marriage that we celebrated on the cruise. Usually that's why people buy gems because they want to represent a milestone in their lives, and that's okay.

It's easy to judge those who have rings on every finger and jewellery draped off of every limb. Some might think their extravagant or boasting their riches, but it may not be that at all. They may have chosen a gem to represent a lost child, or a brother who died in the war, or a hardship they overcame in their life. We don't know their reasoning and we can't presume we do.

Sometimes we see people with tattoos from head to toe. Sometimes the differences in other people stand out so profoundly that we can't help but stare. Yes, I'm talking about myself staring. But I know others stare as well and I'm not the only one. We're all imperfect beings.

But the point I'm trying to get across is that everyone uses markers in some way or another to represent something. It's up to us to dig a little deeper than the surface to see what they're all about. Why does that guy have tattoos from head to toe? Why does that woman have diamonds up and down her ears including piercings in her nose and tongue? These are the questions we should be asking ourselves. I should be asking myself this before I judge anyone.

There is always a reason.

When I think of myself, and think of the reasons that I bought a piece of jewellery or purchased something that means a lot to me, I think of my reasoning behind it and realize that could be somebody else's reason. We've all been through difficult things in our lives, milestones we've overcome, difficult circumstances we've made it through, and that is to be celebrated somehow.

These are the things that bring us worth, that make us who we are. These are our *valuables*. And however people want to represent that, is up to them. You can wear rings on your fingers and bells on your toes, dye your hair blue; you can choose to get a tattoo to represent your friend who died in a car accident, or pierce your tongue because it symbolizes the fact that you finally stopped smoking - and you want to remind yourself of that fact every day.

Regardless of your circumstance, regardless of the pain and sorrow that you've gone through in your life, remember that those are the things that make you who you are and shaped you into the person that God intended you to be. And remembering these things in your life is a good thing; *a great celebration!*

Because these are your *diamonds*, my friends.

These - are your *diamonds!*

Watching Paint Dry

The great Glacier National Park, Alaska is one of the most beautiful places in the world. You can't get there by foot, in fact man has probably never even stepped foot on most of those beautiful mountains dotted with Glaciers.

It was the most breathtaking part of Alaska that we'd ever set eyes on. As we entered into the beautiful oceanic view of the *Marjorie Glacier*, our jaws dropped. We raced to the railing of the ship, taking picture after picture of this spectacular scenery.

There really are no words to explain how beautiful it was.

The ship reached the *Marjorie Glacier* and we hovered there doing a full 360 so that all passengers could see this wonder that God had made. It was blue ice mounded together in such an amazing way. It's like all the liquid was drained out of the giant slab of ice, and all that remained was blue crystals stuck together.

I took many pictures, and when I thought I was done taking pictures, I took some more. And when I was done taking pictures, I took live video footage. I couldn't get enough of it. How can anyone be bored of such beauty?

Well my husband did.

He referred to it as *'watching paint dry.'* As you can imagine I was appalled. "How can you be bored of this?" I questioned him. "It is *so* beautiful!"

I guess thinking about it now, I realize I did overdo the pictures, and videos, and we were out there for quite a long time, so I can see how someone would lose interest. The scenery didn't change while the cruise ship hovered.

I laugh when I think of it now. The analogy to *watching paint dry* was pretty ingenious and funny at the same time. I wonder if that was what God experienced when he made the world in seven days. It's like painting a canvas, and it may well have been like watching paint dry for God.

Can you imagine creating the world?

If you think of an artist painting a picture and creating something from nothing, it's really amazing. The image portrayed in the artist's mind that no one else has ever seen, is original, unique, and one-of-a-kind.

That is our earth, and it is only by God's great miracle that He created such beauty. It's a beauty created from His mind and we get to enjoy it every single day. That's amazing if you think about it. We get to live and breathe in a world that was created by God himself.

Going to Alaska and seeing its beauty, made me realize how many amazing things there really are on this planet.

Yes there's poverty, yes there's war-torn regions and third World countries, and sickness and pain and devastation. But there's also this grandeur, this beauty that we don't even realize is out there. There's so much hidden land that man hasn't even touched, and we never get to see that.

It's God's creation and it's beautiful! You don't quite realize it until you see Alaska, and the breathtaking glaciers like the *Marjorie Glacier* and the mountains surrounding it as well as the blue-green oceans that kiss its icy shore.

So even though my husband refers to it as watching paint dry, I smile at that analogy and I envision God in those seven days painting His canvas, and I'm very proud to have witnessed the masterpiece in the raw.

Cruising to Alaska was the best reminder that God made it *all!* I read Genesis 1 in a different light now, and I appreciate the artist so much more!

Genesis 1-31, *"In the beginning God created the heavens and the earth. Now the earth was formless and empty, darkness was over the surface of the deep, and the Spirit of God was hovering over the waters. And God said, "Let there be light," and there was light. God saw that the light was good, and He separated the light from the darkness. God called the light 'day,' and the darkness He called 'night.' And there was evening, and there was morning – the first day.*

And God said, "Let there be a vault between the waters to separate water from water." So God made the vault and separated the water under the vault from the water above it. And it was so. God called the vault 'sky.' And there was evening, and there was morning – the second day.

And God said, "Let the water under the sky be gathered to one place, and let dry ground appear." And it was so. God called the dry ground 'land' and gathered waters He called 'seas.' And God saw that it was good. Then God said, "Let the land produce vegetation: seed-bearing plants and trees on the land that bear fruit with seed in it, according to their various kinds." And it was so. The land produced vegetation: plants bearing seed according to their kinds and the trees bearing fruit with seed in it according to their kinds. And God saw that it was good. And there was evening, and there was morning – the third day.

And God said, "Let there be lights in the vault of the sky to separate the day from the night, and let them serve as signs to mark sacred times, and days and years, and let them be lights in the vault of the sky to give light on the earth." And it was so. God made two great lights – the greater light to govern the day and the lesser light to govern the night. He also made the stars. God set them in the vault of the sky to give light on the earth, to govern the day and the night, and to separate light from darkness. And God saw that it was good. And there was evening, and there was morning – the fourth day.

And God said, "Let the water team with living creatures, and let birds fly above the earth across the vault of the sky." So God created the great creatures of the sea and every living thing with which the water teems and that moves about in it, according to their kinds, and every winged bird according to its kind. And God saw that it was good. God blessed them and said, "Be fruitful and increase in number and fill the water in the seas, and let the birds increase on the earth." And there was evening, and there was morning—the fifth day.

And God said, "Let the land produce living creatures according to their kinds: the livestock, the creatures that move along the ground, and the wild animals, each according to its kind." And it was so. God made the wild animals according to their kinds, the livestock according to their kinds, and all the creatures *that move along the ground according to their kinds. And God saw that it was good.*

Then God said, "Let us make mankind in our image, in our likeness, so that they may rule over the fish in the sea and the birds in the sky, over the livestock and all the wild animals, and over all the creatures that move along the ground." So God created mankind in His own image, in the image of God He created them; male and female He created them. God blessed them and said to them, "Be fruitful and increase in number; fill the earth and subdue it. Rule over the fish in the sea and the birds in the sky and over every living creature that moves on the ground.

Then God said, "I give you every seed-bearing plant on the face of the whole earth and every tree that has fruit with seed in it. They will be yours for food. And to all the beasts of the earth and all the birds in the sky and all the creatures that move along the ground—everything that has the breath of life in it—I give every green plant for food." And it was so. God saw all that He had made, and it was very good. And there was evening, and there was morning—the sixth day."

And on the seventh day He rested. No doubt the great artist was tired. He made a beautiful world for us to enjoy. I hope to get to see more of His wonderful creation some day but I'm thankful I had the opportunity to witness some of His best work that day in Glacier Bay, Alaska, floating on a ship.

Watching paint dry.

The Last Flight Home

Entitlement, it's something we all struggle with, including myself. We think we have a right to this, and a right to that, and the world should run according to our every whim. Well it doesn't. Firstly, it shouldn't. There are so many different individual stories going on out there, that we couldn't possibly begin to understand the full scheme of things.

But God can, and for that I am completely thankful. But we forget...*easily!*

I experienced a good taste of this on the last flight home from Alaska. We had just made it into the Vancouver airport from Anchorage, in hopes to catch a connecting flight to Saskatoon. We already had the tickets.

The connection was supposed to be easy, but it was anything but that. Originally, on our tickets, it said that we should have a good hour in which to collect our luggage, recheck it, go through customs, and security, and make it to our connecting flight.

Maybe in a perfect world, but this world is far from perfect. I don't know how many times I've expected perfection and became stressed over it. I should know better, right?

Still, I expected everything would work out just wonderful. The plane would arrive on time, we'd collect our luggage from the carousel almost immediately, and have enough time to comfortably find our seats in the connecting flight, let out a breath, and relax.

Call me Pollyanna, but if I can't force the world to be happy and perfect, I'll pretend it is, or I'll write a story making sure of that fact. But realistically, things don't work out like that. People fail us, disappointments happen everyday. We can't stop that, it is what it is. But while this is going on, we have to adjust our brains. Something I forgot to do, that last flight home.

I thought that if I purchased a ticket, that would guarantee me a flight. I thought that was a given, that my vacation would be stress-free, but that wasn't in fine print. In fact, it was only in my head.

Our baggage ended up taking a full forty five minutes to come through the carousel. I don't know why, but I think perhaps people were watching a hockey game on TV. I guess the Stanley Cup was on because people were cheering and jumping up and down watching the screens positioned throughout the airport. My husband and I of course were not sports fans at all so we didn't pay any attention.

It could have been the game, or a myriad of other things going on that we didn't know about, but regardless, our bags were late. And not just ours, everyone's baggage from the Anchorage flight was late.

Now, if you do the math, you'll figure out pretty quickly that our connection flight was about to take off without us. That was not a good thing. I was almost immediately stressed, and worried that we wouldn't have enough time to recheck our bags, go through customs, and security, and we would not be able to get home.

While chatting with others who were waiting at the same time, I soon realized that my life, my husband's life, was not the only life affected in this botched up transit. As I stated in the beginning, there are usually many different stories going on at the same time.

One story in particular, moved me. I met a lady who had cancer and she told me that she could not miss this connection flight because she had an important treatment the next morning in Saskatoon. It was literally life or death for her. We often don't think of others when we go through difficulties. We don't think how our actions can affect others but they do. We all just expect things to happen to benefit *us*.

After all, aren't we entitled to that?

As it turned out, we finally retrieved our baggage and brought it to the gate where we were supposed to board the plane, but to our disappointment the gate had already closed and we were guided to stand in a new line-up.

Quickly, the group of us butt into the front, and explained the situation insisting that we needed to move on through *fast* because the plane was waiting for us. See, this is what we were told. And in response, we were pointed in the direction to run and assured that we would make it on the flight in time.

I looked around for the cancer lady but I couldn't see her. Somehow in the shuffle, we had lost her. She was pushing a trolley of suitcases and couldn't keep up. My heart hurt for her when I couldn't find her. Tears welled in my eyes as both my husband and I dashed down the corridor while pulling our luggage behind us as we headed to re-check our baggage.

Once we checked our baggage, we were told to hurry down another hallway and around the corner. It wasn't very far, they assured us. All we had to do was hurry. We rushed through customs and then through security and were on our way, or so we thought.

It seemed as though the airport staff had directed us the wrong way. Or perhaps we had gone the wrong way ourselves. In the confusion of it all it was hard to figure out what the heck was going on. But of course, it couldn't be our fault. In my arrogance, I am never wrong.

But, on that fateful day, we were playing the blame game, or was it called *The Amazing race?* We ran for what seemed like hours, and I was far ahead of my husband. I couldn't figure out why he couldn't keep up to me. I was carrying a shoulder bag as my carry-on and also my purse, and he was just wheeling a small light-weight carry-on behind himself.

I figured if I was faster than him, that would benefit both of us because I could hold the plane for him. In my dreams. Once again my arrogance got the better of me, but hey, that's nothing unusual.

Finally, we were directed to the right gate and got there out of breath. I could barely speak, I was so exhausted. I made a mental note: *Must lose thirty pounds.* In my younger days, I could do this sprint no problem, but not today. Not after getting up at five in the morning, departing a cruise ship, traveling on a shuttle bus for two hours, and a four-hour flight to reach this point. Catching a connection flight was not supposed to be this hard!

While standing at the gate, the flight attendant told us the plane was pulling away. At that point I had already been bawling, I couldn't take any more stress. I turned to my husband who had finally arrived, and he was out of breath as well. He was also holding up his pants. Annoyed, I looked him over and wondered what the heck was going on.

So many different stories going on at the same time, as I stated before. We often forget about others when it has to do with ourselves. How very selfish I am sometimes. My poor husband was made to take off his belt while going through customs and security, and didn't even have time to put it back on. I didn't know this. He was running as he struggled to keep his pants up the whole time. He was slow because his pants were falling down.

Yes, we can chuckle now. But at the time, it wasn't funny at all.

Looking back, I think of how selfish I was. I didn't think of the many other things that were going on around me, or the other people that were affected by the same story with different angles. The cancer lady, the flight attendants, the pilot. What kind of day were they having?

We were told that the pilot was going to wait for us so the flight attendant directed us down the jet way. Only, when we got to the end of the jet way, we saw the plane close up and pull away without us. Panic rose in my chest. I started to hyperventilate with spurts of crying fits, and my husband told me to calm down. How could I calm down? I thought to myself. Weren't we entitled to a flight home like the ticket said?

Bawling, I explained to the flight attendant that our son was waiting for us, that we couldn't miss this flight, that it was all *their* fault. But now, after the fact, a few other things come to mind.

It was nobody's fault. Things just happen, people are late, connections fail. People disappoint. God is in control of it all. There is nothing we can say or do to prevent that. And when we do things our own way, *we* are the ones that become out of sync.

What if, heaven forbid, we rushed on that flight and it crashed? What if we weren't meant to be on that flight at all? It literally would have been our last flight home. Crazy thinking, I know, but we often don't think of the repercussions of our actions. We just push through our lives thinking we know better than God.

I do this all the time.

It's in situations like this, situations completely out of my control, that make me shake my head and realize it's not up to me. I can't change a single thing in my life. Only God can do that.

And as it turned out, the pilot re-hooked to the jet way just for us, a situation that almost never happens we're told. We boarded the plane while panting from exhaustion, red faced and teary eyed. As we took our seats, we looked out the small window and waved goodbye to our luggage on the tarmac that wasn't so fortunate to make it on the plane with us. Yes, we didn't see that luggage for three days after that, but at least the airport staff had tried.

As the plane shuttled to the runway and we lifted off, we leaned our heads back and let the bird take us to the sky. Once the seatbelt sign went off, we looked around at all the empty seats and noticed most of our group didn't make it on board. A shame. The cancer lady wasn't there.

We were stunned that we made it on the flight and told the flight attendant to thank the pilot. I tried to relax, but I think it took the entire two hour flight home to catch my breath. As we got comfortable in our seats, I started to think.

Would it have been so bad to be delayed in Vancouver for an extra day? Yes, it would have cost more money and inconvenienced us, but that was life. We could have called our son and told him we missed our flight. I don't know why I thought it was the end of the world if we didn't make it on *that* plane.

Either one of us could have had a heart attack from running so hard. So many different scenarios went through my mind until I finally calmed down. And in the end, I realized something profound: *God controls every little detail.*

And then I smiled.

In spite of myself, and all my efforts to control the situation, I wasn't the one in charge. As Proverbs 16:33 clearly states: "*God, not chance, decides what happens in human affairs.*" That to me is a great comfort.

After all, who of us by worrying, can add a single hour to our lives? *"Not I,"* said the silly, out of breath woman, as *she fought back a new surge of tears that made her realize her efforts, her crazy emotional state, and all the unnecessary worry, hadn't helped her at all.*

It was God, smiling down from above, waiting, watching, then gently guiding us home.

As always!

Twirl

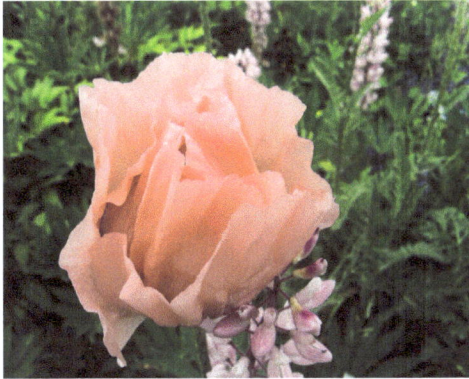

Okay, so I do daring things, I admit that. I like to have fun. My husband doesn't like that part of me I guess. *I scare him.* I don't mean to, it just happens. Ever since we went to Niagara Falls back when we were young newlyweds, I scared the living daylights out of him by stepping on the edge of a railing to take a picture.

I've never lived it down and he's never trusted me in similar situations. I don't blame him, but in my defense, the rail I stood on some twenty-five years ago at Niagara Falls wasn't the only thing between me and a giant waterfall. There was a second railing, and of course I wouldn't step up on that. I'm not *that* crazy.

But Barry doesn't see it that way. He's afraid of heights and it's understandable that it bothers him when I do questionable things. I don't mean to torture him so much.

One of those times happened at the back of the ship during our cruise to Alaska. We were all dressed up after having a lovely meal in the dining room, celebrating our anniversary. We had some time to kill before the Starlight Lounge opened for the evenings performance, so we went out on the promenade deck that wrapped around the entire ship. I loved that deck, and of course the back of the ship was the most daring.

We ventured off there, or should I say, I pulled my reluctant husband by the hand and he had no choice but to follow a crazy woman like me. I wanted to see the motors churning up the sea. It was refreshing and invigorating, not to mention an adrenaline rush, but not so much for my husband.

He was worried.

"Oh c'mon," I told him, "don't be such a big baby."

But he just peeked over the rail for a minute and then clung to the wall. I, on the other hand, loved it. Not only did I love it, I bent over the rail and took pictures and videos. Never at any time did I risk my life or stand on the rail though, just to be clear. I would never be so silly.

After taking pictures, I wanted to do one thing. I had always wanted to twirl around in a full skirt on the deck of a ship like Marilyn Monroe. I don't know why. Call it a crazy childhood fantasy, or just some crazy whim, but I did it.

I stood there at the stern of the ship, against the backdrop of a magnificent ocean sunset, and twirled my heart out despite my poor husband's fear that I was going to suddenly plummet to my death on our first cruise ever.

I feel bad now because I worried my husband, but it was also exhilarating. I did something I always wanted to do.

That to me is worth the risk, albeit a low risk, but you know what I mean. I looked at it as an opportunity to be adventurous. I love adventure and hope I never lose that urge to live and be crazy and laugh and find adventure wherever I am, no matter how old I am.

I want to live a full life and see my dreams come true. And I don't want to just dream; I want to dream *BIG*. I believe Marilyn Monroe dreamed big. She achieved her goals of being a famous actress even though her life didn't end well. That part is sad. But she represents the pursuit of dreams and a chance to give life all that you can, especially with her famous shot of her dress blowing up as she stood above a subway grating on Lexington Avenue in Manhattan so many years ago. Sure it wasn't a twirl, but I'd always envisioned it as one when I was a child and wanted to try it. What girl wouldn't?

I don't ever want to stop having fun, living my heart out, and challenging myself daily. I want to twirl like there was no tomorrow because after all, we are not guaranteed a single day. God doesn't owe us a thing. I always tell myself that it's the other way around. I owe my life to *HIM!*

And so, this is my legacy. When I get to the pearly gates someday and I'm asked what I did with my life, I want to be able to say I *lived!* I made the best of what I had. I loved, and laughed, and enjoyed my life to the fullest! I wasn't afraid to dream and to watch those dreams come true.

I just want to encourage everyone out there to never give up on your dreams no matter what your circumstance. *LIVE, LOVE, LAUGH* as the saying goes. Do what makes you happy, seek God in that happiness, and *TWIRL* my friends.

TWIRL!

The End

ABOUT THE AUTHOR

Award-winning author Kathleen Morris has written numerous articles, poetry, and short stories published in various Saskatchewan newspapers. Her poem *Refuge* is published in a book anthology titled *A Golden Morning*. She has written many plays and skits including her play titled *Gotta Love It*, winner of Dancing Sky Theatre's rural writing contest in 2001 where it was also performed by the theatre troupe in Meacham, Saskatchewan.

Deep Bay Vengeance is Kathleen's first novel followed by its sequel *Deep Bay Relic*. She also writes non-fiction inspirational books about funny stories from her own life. Her latest novel is called *The Prion Attachment,* first book in the *Blood War Trilogy.* When she's not writing, she enjoys spending time with her husband Barry and their three grown children at her home in Saskatchewan, Canada. For more on Kathleen Morris please check out her Amazon Author page at Amazon.com

Other Books By Kathleen Morris

Deep Bay Series
Deep Bay Vengeance
Deep Bay Relic
Deep Bay Legacy (Coming 2014)

Blood War Series
The Prion Attachment
Blood Purge (Coming 2014)

Short Inspirations Series
Size Seven Shorts
Short End Of The Stick
Shortcut To Alaska

Short Stories
Along The Way - 12 Short Stories You Can Read Along
The Way

Plays
Time Will Tell - An Easter Play
Even Me - A Christmas Play For Your Sunday School
All I Need Is Love - A Play For Teens
Lost And Found - A Children's Christmas Play
Gotta Love It - A Humorous Play About Rural Life

How - To Books
How To Make Eye Catching Ebook Covers Easily

Available on Amazon.com

www.ingramcontent.com/pod-product-compliance
Lightning Source LLC
LaVergne TN
LVHW010028070426
835513LV00001B/10